Unleashing the Mindful Creator

Buddha's Teachings on Creativity

Table of Contents

1. Introduction ... 1

2. Setting the Stage: A Brief Introduction to Buddhism ... 2

    2.1. Understanding The Life of Buddha ... 2

    2.2. Understanding The Four Noble Truths ... 2

    2.3. The Noble Eightfold Path ... 3

    2.4. The Concept of Non-Self (Anatta) and Impermanence (Anicca) ... 4

    2.5. Meditation in Buddhism ... 4

    2.6. Diverse Buddhist Traditions ... 5

3. The Zen of Artistry: Buddha's Perception on Creativity ... 6

    3.1. Mindfulness and the Creative Process ... 6

    3.2. Emptiness: The Birthplace of Creativity ... 7

    3.3. Presence over Perfection ... 7

    3.4. Interconnectedness and the 'Enso' ... 8

4. Unveiling The Mindful Creator: Meditation as a Gateway ... 10

    4.1. The Meaning and Significance of Meditation ... 10

    4.2. Meditation and the Creative Mind ... 11

    4.3. The Role of Mindfulness in Creative Enlightenment ... 11

    4.4. Techniques for Harnessing Creative Power through Meditation ... 12

    4.5. Embracing Uncomfortable Emotions: A Catalyst for Creativity ... 12

    4.6. The Creative Consciousness: A Journey, Not a Destination ... 13

5. The Four Noble Truths: Uncovering the Roots of Artistic Struggle ... 14

    5.1. The Noble Truth of Suffering: Dukkha ... 14

    5.2. The Noble Truth of the Cause of Suffering: Samudaya ... 15

    5.3. The Noble Truth of the Cessation of Suffering: Nirodha ... 15

5.4. The Noble Truth of the Path Leading to the Cessation of Suffering: Magga 16

6. The Eightfold Path: A Blueprint for Creative Enlightenment 18

6.1. Understanding the Eightfold Path 18

6.2. Right View and Creativity 18

6.3. Right Intention and Creativity 19

6.4. Right Speech and Creativity 19

6.5. Right Action and Creativity 20

6.6. Right Livelihood and Creativity 20

6.7. Right Effort and Creativity 20

6.8. Right Mindfulness and Creativity 21

6.9. Right Concentration and Creativity 21

7. Buddha's Teachings in Contemporary Creative Practices 23

7.1. Dhamma and Creativity 23

7.2. The Four Noble Truths and The Eightfold Path: Touchstones of Enlightenment and Creativity 24

7.3. Mindfulness as a Tool for Unleashing Creativity 25

7.4. Embracing Impermanence: The Art of "Non-Attachment" in Creativity 26

7.5. Buddha's Teachings and the Power of Creative Collaboration 26

8. Mindfulness and Flow: The Perfect Symmetry 27

8.1. Mindfulness: A Prelude 27

8.2. The Merger of Mindfulness and Creativity 28

8.3. Flow: The Culmination of Mindfulness and Creativity 28

8.4. Exercises for Cultivating Mindfulness and Encouraging Flow 29

8.5. How Buddhism and Psychology Unite Mindfulness, Flow, and Creativity 30

9. Overcoming Creative Blocks Through Buddhist Wisdom 31

9.1. Understanding Creative Blocks 31

9.2. Embracing Impermanence 31

9.3. Acknowledging the 'Three Poisons' 32

9.4. Techniques to Overcome Poisons 33

9.5. Conclusion 33

10. Balancing Creativity and Compassion: Spiritual and Artistic
Growth 35

10.1. Finding the Connection: Creativity and Compassivity 35

10.2. The Importance of Balance 36

10.3. Practical Ways to Balance Creativity and Compassion 36

10.4. Cultivating Compassion through Art Therapy 37

10.5. Creative Outlets for Compassion 37

11. Conclusion: Embracing Your Transformative Creative Journey . 39

11.1. Embrace Impermanence in Creativity 39

11.2. The Power of Mindfulness 39

11.3. The Interplay of Form and Emptiness - The Heart of
Creativity 40

11.4. Embodying Compassion - Infusing Heart Into Your Art 40

11.5. Acceptance and Letting Go - Developing Creative
Resilience 40

11.6. Integrating Creativity in Daily Life - Living Artfully 41

Chapter 1. Introduction

Dive into a refreshing exploration of one's own creative consciousness with our Special Report: "Unleashing the Mindful Creator: Buddha's Teachings on Creativity." This illuminating guide brightly bridges the boundless realms of spirituality and creativity, opening doors to unseen dimensions of inventive thought and artistic expression. Rooted in timeless wisdom, yet aptly suited for the modern-day creator, this report offers an enriching journey into Buddha's teachings and their profound implications on creativity. Whether you're an artist yearning for a deeper connection with your craft or a curious seeker pursuing personal growth and ingenuity, this report promises to uplift, inspire, and cultivate your inherent creative potential. So exhilarate your senses, ignite your imagination, and ready yourself for a vibrant voyage into the mindful landscape of creation!

Chapter 2. Setting the Stage: A Brief Introduction to Buddhism

Buddhism, often described as more philosophy than religion, sprouted from the ancient Indian subcontinent around the 5th or 6th Century BCE. Born from Prince Siddhartha Gautama's pursuit of Enlightenment, Buddhism now blossoms worldwide. Before we explore its intertwining roots with creativity, we will deepen our understanding of Buddhism's essential principles.

2.1. Understanding The Life of Buddha

Siddhartha Gautama, the Buddha, was born in Lumbini (now Nepal) around 563 BCE to a royal family. Living a life of luxury behind palace walls, Siddhartha didn't encounter human suffering until his 20s when he witnessed old age, sickness, and death. Alarmed by the prevalence of suffering, he abandoned his royal life and began seeking Enlightenment to conquer human suffering.

After several years of austere practices and meditation, he attained Enlightenment under the Bodhi tree in Bodh Gaya (India). Enlightened, Siddhartha came to be known as Buddha, meaning 'The Enlightened One.' From here, he began disseminating his profound insights – forming the essence of Buddhist teachings.

2.2. Understanding The Four Noble Truths

Central to Buddhist teachings are the Four Noble Truths, a

foundational framework marking the reality of life and a path leading towards liberation from suffering.

1. **The Truth of Suffering (Dukkha)**: Life inevitably involves suffering. Both physical (illness, aging, death) and mental (frustration, disappointment, despair).

2. **The Truth of the Cause of Suffering (Samudaya)**: Suffering arises from craving or attachment. Desiring to have (greed), to not have (aversion), or not knowing the true nature of things (ignorance) leads to suffering.

3. **The Truth of the End of Suffering (Nirodha)**: There is a cessation of suffering. With the complete end of craving, consequently comes the end of suffering.

4. **The Truth of the Path Leading to the End of Suffering (Magga)**: Following the Eightfold Path can lead to the cessation of suffering.

These truths offer a pragmatic approach towards life, deriving from Buddha's profound meditative insights into the nature of reality. They represent a process of understanding suffering, its roots, the potential for ending suffering, and the path towards its cessation.

2.3. The Noble Eightfold Path

The Noble Eightfold Path, the Fourth Noble Truth, provides a disciplinary guide towards moral, mindfulness, and wisdom-led living to end suffering.

1. **Right Understanding**: Comprehending the Four Noble Truths.

2. **Right Thought**: Nurturing thoughts of detachment, love, and non-violence.

3. **Right Speech**: Abstaining from lies, gossip, hurtful or idle talk.

4. **Right Action**: Avoiding actions causing harm.

5. **Right Livelihood**: Earning a living that does not harm others.

6. **Right Effort**: Cultivating wholesome qualities and shedding unwholesome ones.

7. **Right Mindfulness**: Developing alertness to body, feelings, mind, and phenomena.

8. **Right Concentration**: Cultivating the skill of meditative absorption.

These eight aspects of the path aren't linear stages but interconnected facets of a holistic approach to ethical and mindful living, leading to a deepened understanding of reality and ultimate liberation from suffering.

2.4. The Concept of Non-Self (Anatta) and Impermanence (Anicca)

Buddhism conveys two pivotal concepts - Anatta or non-self and Anicca or impermanence. The former dismisses the notion of a static 'self' or 'soul.' Instead, it proposes that what we perceive as 'self' is a combination of shifting physical and mental phenomena.

Impermanence, on the other hand, highlights the transient nature of all phenomena. Nothing is fixed or eternal, neither joy nor suffering.

2.5. Meditation in Buddhism

Meditation forms a cornerstone of Buddhist practice, aiding followers in developing mindfulness, concentration, and insight. Two main types of meditation in Buddhism are Samatha (calming the mind) and Vipassana (insight into the true nature of reality).

2.6. Diverse Buddhist Traditions

Buddhism branched into several traditions over time, each with distinctive practices and interpretations. The three primary branches include Theravada (The Way of the Elders, prevalent in Southeast Asia), Mahayana (The Great Vehicle, dominant in East Asia), and Vajrayana (Diamond Vehicle or Tibetan Buddhism), each further burgeoning into school divisions based on cultural variations and differences in scriptural interpretations.

While Theravada is known for its strict adherence to early texts and monastic discipline, Mahayana emphasizes the universal potential for Buddhahood, and Vajrayana integrates tantric practices to accelerate Enlightenment. Regardless of the differences, the core principles of understanding the nature of reality and mitigation of suffering pervade all traditions.

In essence, Buddhism is a transformative practice focusing on moral discipline, mindfulness, and wisdom to apprehend the true nature of reality, ultimately leading to the cessation of suffering and the attainment of Enlightenment. Its teachings hold immense relevance today, offering practical solutions to alleviate personal and societal suffering. As we move forward in our exploration of creativity through the Buddhist lens, these principles will guide our understanding and inspire us to weave the essence of Buddhist teachings into our creative ventures.

Chapter 3. The Zen of Artistry: Buddha's Perception on Creativity

Artistry can be seen as the ultimate celebration of human existence – a pure expression of our most profound thoughts, emotions, and experiences. For the Buddha, it was more than an aesthetic pursuit; it was a path of mindfulness, a practice of presence, and a gateway to enlightenment. This chapter delves into the intersection of Zen and artistry, offering a fresh perspective on how Buddha's teachings can illuminate your creative journey.

3.1. Mindfulness and the Creative Process

Many creatives describe their most rewarding moments as those when they lose themselves in the flow of creation, when the chatter of the mind fades away and they are present fully, and solely, in the act of making. This is a testament to the deep connection between mindfulness and creativity.

Mindfulness, as taught by Buddha, is about fostering awareness of the present moment, accepting it without judgement, and fully engaging in whatever experience we are having. When applied to the creative process, it's about being completely absorbed in the ongoing evolution of your artwork. Letting our awareness rest fully on the act of creating allows us to connect more deeply with our inner creative energy.

Every brushstroke, every note played, every word written, becomes an act of mindful attention. We become attuned to the subtle interplay of ideas and emotions, and the ordinary linear flow of time seems to fall away. The more we practice mindfulness, the more readily we can slip into this state of 'creative flow'.

3.2. Emptiness: The Birthplace of Creativity

Central to Buddha's teachings is the concept of emptiness, which plays a critical role in understanding the nature of creativity. Emptiness does not denote absence or void, as often misunderstood; rather, it represents the state of potential, the unmanifest source from where all creative expressions arise.

In Buddhist teachings, form is born of emptiness, just as creativity springs from a quiet mind. When the mind is stilled, rid of distracting thoughts and impressions, we create room for new ideas and inspirations to arise. This empty space is not 'nothing', it is the fertile ground for 'everything' that is yet to be created.

Practicing meditative techniques like mindfulness can help quiet the mind and cultivate this inner spaciousness. This, in turn, can unlock the door to infinite creative possibilities.

3.3. Presence over Perfection

Striving for perfection can restrict creativity. Instead, embracing the concept of 'presence over perfection' can liberate the artistic spirit. Buddha said, "Do not dwell in the past, do not dream of the future, concentrate the mind on the present moment." If we apply this wisdom to artistry, it guides us to focus not on the final artwork, but on the process of creation itself.

An artist embarks on a journey with each creation. Every step - from the conception to the completion - is a unique experience of its own, and each one has its worth. Slowing down, being present and finding joy in the process of creating rather than treating it as a means to an end shifts our focus from trying to achieve perfection to experiencing and expressing our authenticity.

3.4. Interconnectedness and the 'Enso'

Buddha's teachings emphasize the interrelatedness of all things. In the artistic universe, this interconnectedness is often symbolized by the 'Enso', a hand-drawn circle in one or two brushstrokes. This Japanese Zen symbol embodies the unity and completeness of the universe.

The Enso signifies that everything (the artist, the artwork, the audience) is interconnected in the grand creative dance of the universe. Understanding this concept underscores that each artistic expression is not just an isolated event. It is an intimate part of an ongoing dialogue with the viewer and the universe at large.

By recognizing this interconnectedness, we can break free of the limits of individuality and isolation, culminating in a freer, more enlightened form of creativity. This wider perspective can enable us to channel artistry that truly touches lives and transforms perceptions, conjuring an aesthetic experience that is shared, felt, and cherished in the collective human experience.

Each phase of artistry - from conception to creation and reception - becomes an integral element in the continuum of creative energy. Our art, therefore, emanates not just from the mind but from the heart, resonating deeply with others and contributing to the collective consciousness.

This deep dive into mindfulness, emptiness, focusing on presence over perfection, and the interconnectedness of all things reveals the profound layers of Buddha's perception on creativity. Like the infinite strokes in a Zen painting, understanding, comprehending, and applying these teachings is an enlightening journey in itself. The path of the mindful creator is not a finite destination, but an ongoing voyage of discovery, where each artistic endeavor becomes a stepping stone towards self-realization and spiritual growth. By embracing Buddha's teachings on creativity, we can enrich our creative pursuits, transforming them into potent instruments of self-discovery, mindfulness, and positive change.

Chapter 4. Unveiling The Mindful Creator: Meditation as a Gateway

Meditation has been universally recognized as a means to encourage tranquility, peace, and spiritual growth. However, within the quiet sanctuary of contemplative meditation, there also exists a potent channel to unmask and cultivate creativity. Through an exploration of the practice and its applications—as drawn from the teachings of Buddha, current research studies and anecdotal examples— this chapter will elucidate how meditation can serve as an extraordinary gateway to liberating the mindful creator within each of us.

4.1. The Meaning and Significance of Meditation

Meditation, in its simplest form, is a mental exercise that focuses on breath, a mantra, an object, or simply awareness of one's thoughts and feelings, fostering a state of relaxation and mental calm. Nestled within this concept is an array of techniques and practices, each offering varied paths to inner peace, mindfulness, and ultimately, untapped creative insight.

But what does meditation truly signify in the context of creativity? And how does it align with Buddha's teachings? The answers lie in Anaapanasati, the Buddhist practice of mindfulness of inhalation and exhalation, leading to insights into the nature of the mind and reality, including their impermanent, unsatisfactory, and unsubstantial nature. This introspective journey opens a gateway into the realm of imagination, fostering a mental state conducive to unveiling creative aptitude.

4.2. Meditation and the Creative Mind

Creativity is often mistakingly pigeonholed as a trait exclusive to specific professions such as artists, writers, or musicians. Yet, it is a fundamental human ability, an inherent part of the fabric that makes up our consciousness. It's the capacity to generate new, innovative, and valuable ideas, beneficial in all aspects of life, from problem-solving in daily life to brainstorming ground-breaking scientific theories.

In this context, meditation is the key to unlocking this creative potential. When one meditates, the mind enters a state of heightened awareness and focus. This mental clarity clears the deck for submerged ideas and innovative thoughts to surface, permeating our consciousness and offering a fertile ground for creativity.

Stories of artists, musicians, and inventors who have discovered breakthrough ideas during or post-meditation abound. Their experiences back the scientific findings that suggest sharper attentiveness to detail, richer sensory experience, and heightened awareness of one's surroundings—factors essential to creative ideation—are among the many benefits of a regular meditation practice.

4.3. The Role of Mindfulness in Creative Enlightenment

Mindfulness, a core concept in Buddha's teachings, is an integral part of meditation that holds the key to a deeper, more profound understanding of creativity. It encourages the practitioner to stay in the present moment, observing thoughts and feelings without judgment or fears of the past or future.

From a creativity perspective, mindfulness promotes openness and flexibility—qualities vital for the generation of novel ideas. It encourages us to see the world from different angles, challenging conventional ways of thinking and opening our minds to unexplored avenues of thought.

4.4. Techniques for Harnessing Creative Power through Meditation

Adopting a suitable meditation technique is paramount to smoothing one's path on this creative voyage. Multiple methods can be adapted and personalized, but a few general pointers merit consideration.

A good starting point is choosing a quiet location devoid of distractions. Sit or lie comfortably, closing your eyes to further minimize external distractions. Pay attention to your breath, focusing on inhalation and exhalation—the basic principal of Anaapanasati—or chant a mantra that resonates with you.

Consistently engage in this practice, and you'll begin to notice a shift in your awareness, heightened focus, and the surfacing of a wellspring of creative ideas—crystalline fragments that together form the vibrant mosaic of your inventive thoughts.

4.5. Embracing Uncomfortable Emotions: A Catalyst for Creativity

At times, meditation may bring up uncomfortable emotions, but these moments carry substantial significance. Dwelling in discomfort and silence often serves as a catalyst to a surge of creativity. Rather than shying away from such feelings, embracing and contemplating them can kindle the spark of unique, transformative ideas.

4.6. The Creative Consciousness: A Journey, Not a Destination

By facilitating a state of mindful presence, meditation carves an unparalleled pathway to the mindful creator within each of us. Yet, it's important to remember that this journey into our creative consciousness is not a destination, but a process that continues to evolve, offering fascinating revelations at each bend.

Though rudimentary and simple at its core, the profundity and immense potential it embodies is limitless. All it takes is a willing heart, a tranquil mind, and a sprouting seed of curiosity to unveil the creative enlightenment that lies within, patiently awaiting discovery. Remember, this journey is yours alone, shaped by your insights, experiences, and revelations, making it a uniquely enriching, endlessly rewarding exploration of your very soul.

Chapter 5. The Four Noble Truths: Uncovering the Roots of Artistic Struggle

In the heart of Buddhism, we encounter The Four Noble Truths - pivotal elements that guide our understanding of life's experiences, like suffering, its causes, the path that leads to cessation of this suffering, and the cessation of suffering itself. For a creator, these truths can be an enlightening path towards uncovering the roots of artistic struggle, examining their sources, and discovering pathways to alleviate them.

5.1. The Noble Truth of Suffering: Dukkha

As artistically inclined beings, we often experience 'Dukkha,' the first Noble Truth. Dukkha, unlike the Western conception of suffering, encompasses a broad range of discomfort from the most trivial to the most profound. It's not just physical or emotional pain, but also unsatisfactoriness, imperfection, impermanence, emptiness, and insubstantiality. As creators, we may confront Dukkha as creative block, dissatisfaction with our work, or the ephemeral nature of inspiration.

Unresolved creative obstacles can trigger a sense of 'tanhā' or thirst. It is yearning for inspiration, for that moment when the brush unabashedly dances on the canvas, words flow onto the paper, or when music spontaneously springs from silence. Recognizing this inconvenience as intricate to the artistic process is to understand the life truth Buddha illuminates. Acknowledge your struggle as Dukkha - this is the first step towards overcoming it.

5.2. The Noble Truth of the Cause of Suffering: Samudaya

The second Noble Truth, 'Samudaya,' pinpoints the origin of suffering. Frequently, the root cause of artistic agony traces back to our inherent 'desire' or thirst. It's crucial to distinguish here that desire themselves are not the issue, chiefly when they propel us towards creative betterment. However, issues arise when these desires become cravings – an intense longing for accomplishment, recognition, or a favorable reception of our artistic output.

Previously held notions and ideals about creativity often induce a strict mind-network that barricades fresh influences. Insights only break through when we open these mental barriers. Untangle them, question them, and see where they're rooted. Understanding these cravings and their roots subverts their power, effectively aligning our minds towards peaceful creativity.

5.3. The Noble Truth of the Cessation of Suffering: Nirodha

The third Noble Truth, 'Nirodha,' teaches us the cessation of suffering. The key is to rein in unbridled 'desires' and 'cravings'. It doesn't necessarily involve suppressing or ostracizing these desires but addressing them mindfully. Channel them through the medium of your art. Treat them as raw material: mold them, shape them, create from them.

This revolutionary thought makes profound sense in a creative context. Indulge in the joy of creating, rather than banking on external validation. Embrace your unique style and allow it to evolve naturally instead of forcing it into preconceived molds. Experience your art, don't just create it.

When perceivable outcomes cease to govern the creative process, liberation ensues. We learn to flow with the journey, focusing less on the end and more on the now. In these absorbed moments, we encounter 'Nirodha' — the cessation of suffering and liberation of creativity.

5.4. The Noble Truth of the Path Leading to the Cessation of Suffering: Magga

Understanding and acknowledging the first three Noble Truths prepares us for 'Magga,' the Fourth Noble Truth—the path leading to the cessation of suffering. This path, often referred to as the Middle Way or the Eightfold Path, guides us to lead balanced lives, not leaning excessively towards self-indulgence or self-denial.

As artists, we can interpret this as maintaining a balance between complete absorption in our art and withdrawal for rejuvenation. Infuse mindfulness in every stroke, every note, every word you craft. Engage with your canvas, manuscript, or instrument as an extension of your being. At the same time, distance yourself periodically to refresh your perspective, to allow new ideas to ferment.

Walk the Middle Way by balancing dedication and disattachment, intuition and intellect, ambition and acceptance. Embrace patience, persistence, and a keen openness to think beyond the conventional. This path is not a quick solution but a journey of self-rediscovery and continual growth. Navigating through this path illuminates the roots of our artistic struggles, transforming them into launching pads for creative liberation and enlightenment.

The Four Noble Truths, thus, serve not only as a primer to Buddhism but also as a profound blueprint to navigate the lanes of creativity and artistic endeavor. Awareness and application of these truths aid a creator in understanding their struggles better and provide tools for transformative action. Through this exploration, we delve deeper into our creative consciousness and unlock doors to unleash our mindful creator—a journey from artistic struggle to enlightened creation.

Chapter 6. The Eightfold Path: A Blueprint for Creative Enlightenment

The Buddha's Eightfold Path provides a principled way forward, a compass leading to awakened living and compassionate interaction with the world. When applied to the creative process, it offers profound, practical guidance.

6.1. Understanding the Eightfold Path

The Eightfold Path as directed by Buddha is as a series of eight interconnected practices or paths: Right View, Right Intention, Right Speech, Right Action, Right Livelihood, Right Effort, Right Mindfulness, and Right Concentration. These are not sequential steps, but integrated practices that weave together to form a comprehensive approach to spiritual and creative development.

Buddha intended these to be followed and developed together, as they work together to lead anyone on the path to enlightenment. This understanding lays the foundation for the individual ways we shall apply these principles to the creativity in the rest of this chapter.

6.2. Right View and Creativity

Right View, also known as Right Understanding, refers to the discernment of seeing the world and everything within it as it genuinely is. Crucial to the creator, it involves understanding impermanence, suffering, and non-self.

In the realm of creativity, Right View helps to understand ideas, tools, techniques, and materials in their actual nature and potential. This can result in a more honest and organic creation that resonates with the creator and the audience. Thus, it can become the foundation for an authentic creative expression.

6.3. Right Intention and Creativity

Right Intention, also referred to as Right Thought or Right Resolve, pertains to the commitment to ethical and mental self-improvement. This principle asks creators to consciously enter their process with clear intentions - to create, not for ego gratification, but for conveying emotions, imparting wisdom, fostering connection, or evoking thought and discussion.

By aligning intentions with the values of compassion, generosity, and empathy, creators can sustain their practice, navigate creative challenges, and wed their work to the greater good. Right Intention infuses a creation with purpose and heart, resonating deeply with the audience.

6.4. Right Speech and Creativity

In the context of Buddha's teachings, Right Speech involves speaking truthfully, kindly, and helpful without resorting to divisive or harsh language. When approached creatively, it is about the honest and ethical communication of one's creative expression.

It's not only about the words used in a creation but also how creators articulate their ideas and messages. For creators who use language as their medium, it emphasizes authenticity, clarity, and respect for the audience, making their work naturally engaging and compelling.

6.5. Right Action and Creativity

Right Action involves conducting oneself in a way that is ethical, non-harming, and responsible. For the creator, it encapsulates the way they engage with their work and the wider world.

Whether sourcing materials, interacting with colleagues, or considering the impact of their output, creators can embody Right Action by fostering a practice rooted in real-world empathy and ethical awareness. This principle serves to deepen the creator's relationship with their craft, audience, and the broader creative ecosystem.

6.6. Right Livelihood and Creativity

The Buddha taught that one's way of life should be morally sound. This, in creativity, is Right Livelihood. Creators must consider whether their practice aligns with their moral and ethical compass.

This might involve considering the implications and impacts of one's creative output on society or the environment or revisiting one's alignment with ethical issues in the creative industry. Right Livelihood also respects creativity itself, seeing it as a nourishing and worthwhile endeavor, rather than a means to an end.

6.7. Right Effort and Creativity

Right Effort, in the context of creativity, is about fostering positive creative habits, maintaining a consistent practice, and cultivating a positive mindset that embraces creative challenges.

This can manifest as dedicating regular time to practice, learning new methods, seeking feedback, celebrating progress, and accepting setbacks as opportunities for learning. It's about perseverance, patience, and commitment to the creative journey, despite its difficulties.

6.8. Right Mindfulness and Creativity

Right Mindfulness in creativity refers to being fully present in the creative moment, aware of physical sensations, thoughts, and emotions that arise during the process. For the creator, it represents the ability to immerse oneself in the creative process with full engagement and conscious observation.

Practising Mindfulness enables creators to tap deep into their impulses, ideas, and emotions, fostering a more intimate understanding of their creative energy. It also helps creators to respond with clarity and calmness to the challenges that arise during the creative process, providing them with a deeper connection with their creativity.

6.9. Right Concentration and Creativity

Right Concentration focuses on mental discipline achieved through practices such as meditation. In a creative context, it encourages deep, uninterrupted immersion in a creative task.

Through meditation, a creator can learn to stabilize their mind, cultivate singular focus, and engage deeply with their work at hand. This kind of creative 'flow' enables a performance peak where a creator connects profoundly with their craft, often leading to innovation and a high standard of work.

The Buddha's Eightfold Path, when interpreted in the context of creativity, provides a blueprint for artists seeking to deepen their creative practice and live more wholly within their creations. The path asks not just for creation, but for mindful creation that imbues life and work with meaning, connection, and a genuine sense of fulfilment. By integrating these eight practices into the creative process, you open the door to newfound artistic insights, a more profound creative connection, and, ultimately, creative enlightenment. Thus, the Eightfold Path provides a comprehensive journey towards a creative life enriched with mindfulness and loftiness of purpose.

Chapter 7. Buddha's Teachings in Contemporary Creative Practices

Buddha's teachings, also known as 'Dhamma', have taken many forms and interpretations throughout the centuries, finding residence in various domains of human experience—one such domain, as we delve in this chapter, is the exponentially expanding sphere of contemporary creative practices.

7.1. Dhamma and Creativity

Understanding the interconnectedness of Dhamma and creativity requires viewing creativity not merely as an act of producing aesthetic or innovative work but as a way of life. In Buddhist philosophy, the mind is the source of all creativity—it is in the mind that thoughts arise, ideas take shape, and creative inspirations are birthed. The Dhamma, being all about mind, mindfulness, and consciousness helps us not only harness the creative power within us but also understand how and why it emerges.

Buddha professed, "The mind is everything. What you think, you become." A powerful assertion that underscores a direct correlation between our internal thought processes and our external realities. By conditioning our minds to see without bias, to understand without judgment, and to imagine without boundaries, we can heighten our creative faculties and contribute to the pool of contemporary creations in more meaningful ways.

7.2. The Four Noble Truths and The Eightfold Path: Touchstones of Enlightenment and Creativity

At the heart of Buddhism are the Four Noble Truths: 1. The truth of suffering (Dukkha) 2. The truth of the cause of suffering (Samudaya) 3. The truth of the end of suffering (Nirodha) 4. The truth of the path that leads to the end of suffering (Magga)

The novel interpretations of these truths in the context of creativity can provide profound insights. Creativity, in many ways, can be viewed as a response to 'Dukkha' or the intrinsic unsatisfactoriness pervading all forms of existence. Our restless search for beauty, expression, novelty, and effect is in itself a reflection of our innate desire to transcend the banal, the ugly, the outdated, and the ineffective.

The second truth, Samudaya, discusses desire or 'tanha' as the cause of suffering. In the realm of creativity, these desires are our attachments to particular ideas, styles, or outcomes that become roadblocks to fluid and unrestricted creative expression. Liberation from these creative blockages comes through 'Nirodha', the cessation of suffering, which entails letting go of rigid attachments.

And finally, we arrive at 'Magga', the path leading to the cease of suffering. Buddha provided an explicit guide in the form of the 'Eightfold Path' that can also parallel the journey of creators.

1. Right Understanding: Comprehending creativity both as a process and a result

2. Right Intent: Fostering intentions that lean towards growth and enrichment rather than mundane achievements

3. Right Speech: Constructive communication about your creative work fostering a collaborative and supportive environment

4. Right Action: Actions manifesting in tune with the creative intent

5. Right Livelihood: Aligning professional activities with one's creative ethos

6. Right Effort: Consistent efforts to hone creative skills and produce authentic work

7. Right Mindfulness: Enhancing creative acuity by being in the moment

8. Right Concentration: Cultivating deep focus that leads to creative breakthroughs

7.3. Mindfulness as a Tool for Unleashing Creativity

One of the most significant teachings of Buddha, mindfulness, provides a robust, practical tool that can be applied directly into everyone's journey of creativity. Mindfulness is the quality of being present, aware of where we are and what we're doing, and not overly reactive or overwhelmed by what's happening around us.

To practice mindfulness in creativity, pay close attention to your thoughts, feelings, and environment as you engage in your creative activities. Observe the way colors coalesce on a canvas, or the rhythm of your fingers dancing on a keyboard, or the subtle tone shifts in music—relish in each moment as it unfolds. Besides enhancing the quality of creative output, mindfulness fosters resilience in the face of creative blocks and the inevitable oscillations of inspiration.

7.4. Embracing Impermanence: The Art of "Non-Attachment" in Creativity

Another fundamental Buddhist teaching that can significantly enhance one's creative journey is the concept of 'Anicca', or impermanence. It means understanding that nothing is static. Change is the only constant. By recognizing and embracing this, creators become capable of evolving their craft without clinging to a particular style, idea, or success. As a result, they find more freedom, resilience, and adaptability in their practice.

7.5. Buddha's Teachings and the Power of Creative Collaboration

Buddha's teachings on compassion, loving-kindness (Metta), and interconnectedness promote empathy and understanding, and can prove transformative when applied to collaborative creative projects. They help shape environments where ideas are freely shared, constructive feedback is nurtured, and collective creativity is enhanced.

To conclude, Buddha's teachings, when transcended into the realm of contemporary creativity, lay the groundwork for a vibrant, mindful, and enriched creative journey. By being mindful creators, we can engage in a transformative ongoing process of creation where the lines between the creator, the process, and the creation blur, allowing us to truly 'become' the art. Every act, thought, word, and moment then become pieces of this ever-unfolding masterpiece. Thus, we do not merely 'create'; we 'live' creativity. The circle of creativity and mindfulness go on—endlessly inspiring, endlessly created.

Chapter 8. Mindfulness and Flow: The Perfect Symmetry

The enlightening teachings of Buddha speak extensively about mindfulness, a concept central to his philosophy. Accordingly, creativity - an unfolding of the unfathomable human mind - shares a profound connection with mindfulness. When they work symbiotically, they engender 'Flow', a state transcending the ordinary spheres of consciousness. This could be envisioned as sailing in an invigorating current of creative energy that merges your awareness with the actions you carry out.

8.1. Mindfulness: A Prelude

Mindfulness, in its simplest form, is the focused and fully engaged attention on the present. It's the clear discernment of what is happening around us and within us at every moment, without any impulsions to alter the reality as it unravels. Buddha emphasized mindfulness as both the key to the understanding of life processes and the path towards liberation from the afflictive cycles of human existence.

In his seminal lecture, "The Foundations of Mindfulness", the Buddha elucidated the four foundations of mindfulness: body (awareness of physical sensations), feelings (awareness of emotional responses), mind (awareness of mental states), and Dhamma (awareness of the reality of phenomena). The practice, also known as 'satipatthana', is vital in maintaining equanimity amidst the unavoidable ebb and flow of life experiences.

8.2. The Merger of Mindfulness and Creativity

Creativity, an innate human propensity, is the capacity to generate, perceive, or appreciate new and valuable ideas, solutions, or artistic expressions. Despite its often spontaneous appearance, creativity can be fostered and amplified by regularly immersing oneself in a conducive mental state.

When married to mindfulness, creativity enjoys an added vigor. Being present and open, without judgment, affords us the mental space essential to the nurturing of creativity. Mindfulness dispels the clutter of distraction, stressors, or confined thinking patterns, permitting the mind to wander freely in the pristine terrains of inspiration. It becomes the thriving soil from where the seeds of novel ideas emerge and flourish.

The mindfulness-creativity synergy necessitates that we attune our intuitive sensors to the subtlest nuances of our physical reality and emotional landscape, absorb experiences fully, perceive connections between seemingly disconnected elements, and venture beyond normative thinking constraints into unknown realms of artistic endeavor.

8.3. Flow: The Culmination of Mindfulness and Creativity

Renowned psychologist Mihaly Csikszentmihalyi introduced the concept of 'Flow', defining it as a state of profound immersion in an activity that produces intense focus, resulting in a heightened sense of satisfaction and fulfillment. In the Flow state, we experience time dilation, lose self-consciousness, and summon an almost effortless surge of creativity.

The achievement of this harmonious state is strikingly reminiscent of mindfulness practice - a perfect symmetry indeed. Both require a deep, unbroken focus on the task at hand, an openness to the emerging experience, and an intrinsic motivation to engage with the process. When engaged in a flow state, you're invoking mindfulness without conscious deliberation.

The connection of flow, mindfulness, and creativity constructs a rewarding cyclical process. Creativity induces the motivation to engage in creative activities. Mindfulness amplifies the focus and openness in these activities, leading to flow, which in turn increases satisfaction, reinforcing the initial motivation for creativity. This mindful-flow loop can become a powerful force driving creativity and personal well-being.

8.4. Exercises for Cultivating Mindfulness and Encouraging Flow

Here are some exercises to foster mindfulness and induce flow states:

- **Focused Breathing:** Allocate time each day to observe your breath's rhythmic passage, noting its dance as it flows in and out.

- **Immersey in Nature:** Engage without distraction in the sensory exploration of nature, taking note of the sounds, sights, smells, textures, and tastes.

- **Nonjudgmental Observation:** Pay close attention to your thoughts and feelings without reacting to them or judging them.

- **Complete Immersion:** Engage wholly with creative tasks at hand without concern for the outcome but simply for the joy of the process.

8.5. How Buddhism and Psychology Unite Mindfulness, Flow, and Creativity

Through Buddha's teachings, we understand that mindfulness brings about mental clarity, tranquility, and a heightened mental presence. Concurrently, in psychology, flow represents an optimal state ideal for creativity's efflorescence. By uniting these philosophies, we can undoubtedly wade into a profound understanding of our creative impulses and potentially unlock an unprecedented scale of artistic expression and fulfillment.

Mindfulness and flow together pave the path that allows liminal thinking to transpire, helping creators surpass their creative limitations and foster self-awareness, insight, and empathy. This mental state encourages the creator to probe deeper into the recesses of the self and the universe, sparking innovation powered by wisdom and compassion – the very bedrock of creative mindfulness.

As we thread through these insights, we might observe that creativity rests not merely as an outcome but the journey itself, an exploration of the multitude of possibilities reflecting the boundless potential of the human mind. As Buddha communicated, mindfulness and awareness are the steps towards enlightenment—when applied to our creative pursuits, we can attain a riveting personal understanding of our artistic self, launching us into an elevated paradigm of existence where creativity and spirituality coalesce in harmonious resonance. The exploration of the mindfulness-creativity-flow relationship is not only profoundly illuminating but potentially life-changing in its integration into our daily lives.

Chapter 9. Overcoming Creative Blocks Through Buddhist Wisdom

Creative stumbling blocks: those invisible barriers that silently creep up on us, eroding our confidence and stifiling our inventiveness. They create a maddening hamster wheel of constant repetitive thoughts and nullify any creative spark that even slightly glimmers. The burning question arises: Where has our fountain of creativity vanished? The answer swathed in the wisdom of Buddhism, shines a spotlight on using instinctive mindfulness in subduing these irritating intruders.

9.1. Understanding Creative Blocks

The understanding of creative blocks from a Buddhist perspective begins with the principle of 'Anicca' - the impermanence of all things. As creativity ebbs and flows, so do blocks. They are not a fixed state that remains eternally, rather they flicker in and out of existence, often powered by our own perception and awareness.

But why do these blocks happen? The Buddha's teachings reveal that blocks are formed through three main afflictions known as 'The Three Poisons'; these include Ignorance (Moha), Attachment (Raga) and Aversion (Dwesha). Ignorance misleads, Attachment binds to old ideas and past successes, while Aversion adamantly resists change and new ideas. Thus, creative blocks arise, creating a seeming desert of inspiration.

9.2. Embracing Impermanence

Creativity by its very nature is not designed to be a static, monotonous stream, but a dynamic flow of ebbs and surges. In Buddhist philosophy, embracing 'Anicca' or the principle of impermanence inspires one to view these temporary periods of dry creativity not as an enduring predicament but rather a passing phase. This changes the relationship we share with our creative blocks, from one of dread and dismay to a relationship of understanding and patience.

When we learn to dance with the rhythm of impermanence, we welcome every stage of our creative journey, blocks included. They are no longer our enemies but stepping stones toward achieving a richer creative intellect and deeper mindfulness.

9.3. Acknowledging the 'Three Poisons'

To overcome our blocks, we must first identify their roots. In Buddhist philosophy, the 'Three Poisons' of Ignorance, Attachment, and Aversion often turn out to be the culprits behind our creative blocks.

- Ignorance, the first poison, dims our awareness, obscures our innate wisdom, and numbs us to new, potentially thriving, ideas.

- The second poison, Attachment, binds us to old patterns, compelling us to replicate past successes instead of progressing toward uncharted territories of creativity.

- Lastly, Aversion repels unfamiliar or challenging ideas. To favor comfort over growth, we resist changes and opportunities.

By gaining cognizance of these root causes, we initiate the process of recovery and creative rejuvenation.

9.4. Techniques to Overcome Poisons

Having identified the poisons, let's delve into the strategies to counter their debilitating effects:

1. **Stillness meditation:** also known as 'Shamatha', it brings our thoughts and emotions under control, providing much-needed tranquility in the storm of creative blocks.

2. **Insight meditation:** named 'Vipassana', it gradually uncovers the roots of our creative blocks, deeply embedded in our subconscious.

3. **Metta meditation:** or the practice of immeasurable love and compassion, diverts our focus from our blocks and wards off negativity and self-deprecating thoughts.

These interactions with the mind, meditation in essence, provide illumination in the darkness of creative blocks.

Then about cultivating detachment and acceptance; this aids in releasing the grip of the fetters 'Raga' (Attachment) and 'Dwesha' (Aversion), allowing for a free flow of fresh and inventive ideas.

9.5. Conclusion

In the end, it all boils down to viewing your creative life through the lens of Buddhist wisdom. Remember that creative blocks are impermanent and can be a welcoming space for introspection. Do not dread or resist them but patiently dance along. Know that they arise from Ignorance, Attachment, and Aversion, and these 'poisons' can be combated with attuned mindfulness and practicing stillness, insight and Metta meditations.

By incorporating these teachings, we can mindfully sweep away the cobwebs of stagnation and invite the dawn of unrestrained creativity. This encourages not just creative revitalization but also inner peace, tranquility, and personal enlightenment. So the next time creative blocks loom up, approach them with the light of Buddhist tenets, and watch as they crumble, setting your creativity free.

Chapter 10. Balancing Creativity and Compassion: Spiritual and Artistic Growth

In a quiet and serene space of the mind, one can find a delicate balance between creativity and compassion—a powerful dynamic essential to both spiritual and artistic growth. As Buddha taught, the path to enlightenment lies in the Middle Way, which fundamentally pertains to balance. It is this harmony between divergent forces that serves as the key to unlocking the vast, untapped potential of the mind. This concept has incredible implications for individual growth and realization, especially in the realms of creativity and compassion.

10.1. Finding the Connection: Creativity and Compassivity

Creativity and compassion appear initially to be two differing paradigms. However, when inspected closely, they share a profound, symbiotic relationship echoed in Buddhist philosophy. The Buddha held that dependent origination, or the interconnectedness of all things and the law of cause and effect, forms the web on which each creative and compassionate act spins. In other words, when we engage in acts of compassion, we pave the way for the birth of profound creativity, and the resulting creative outputs, in turn, provoke feelings and acts of compassion.

The idea of seeing and creating art can undoubtedly be linked to the idea of compassion — the feeling of deep sympathy and sorrow for another who is stricken by misfortune, accompanied by a strong desire to alleviate that suffering. When we create or engage with art, we create and share continually changing narratives, reflections of our life's passions, sufferings, and joys. This interpretive journey into art forms cultivates profound compassion—for the artist, for self, and for others who may relate to the artistic interpretation.

10.2. The Importance of Balance

Finding the correct balance between creativity and compassion is of utmost importance. Excess creativity sans compassion may lead to art devoid of sensitivity, and too much compassion without creativity can become overwhelming, stifling one's ability to express. Striking the right balance, much like Buddha's Middle Way, liberates the mind, enriching spiritual and artistic growth. The Buddha urged one to avoid extremes and follow a path of moderation. This philosophy of balance carries incredible importance when applied to understanding the mutual relationship between creativity and compassion, which are interconnected and concurrently fueled.

10.3. Practical Ways to Balance Creativity and Compassion

We can encourage the helpful interplay of creativity and compassion by blending practices that enhance our ability to deepen in both areas.

1. **Mindfulness**: Start practicing mindfulness. Being fully present and immersed in moments enables a deeper connection with oneself and others, forming the bedrock of compassion and creative expression.

2. **Meditation**: The practice of meditation, in particular, loving-kindness meditation exercises can help foster a strong sense of compassion. Studies show a gentle but significant boost in creativity following loving-kindness meditation.

3. **Active Art Creation**: Push boundaries and explore different

forms of art to keep creativity alive; this can be writing, painting, dancing, or music. Art offers an expressive outlet for compassion to flow freely.

4. **Engage in Art Appreciation**: Art appreciation develops a profound understanding of different perspectives, promoting empathy and compassion.

10.4. Cultivating Compassion through Art Therapy

Art offers great potential as a catalyst for cultivating compassion. It creates a safe space where people can freely express complex thoughts, emotions, and experiences that are often hard to articulate through words alone. Art becomes a channel through which an individual can empathize and understand the experiences of others, further fueling compassion.

Art therapy is a powerful tool that encompasses activities such as painting, drawing, and sculpting. It allows individuals to explore their emotions and improve self-esteem, self-awareness, and cultivate compassion.

10.5. Creative Outlets for Compassion

Buddhist teachings emphasize the importance of active compassion or 'Karuna'. This action-driven compassion motivates us to alleviate suffering and promote happiness in others' lives. Creativity intertwined with compassion often results in activities that not only reflect but also respond to the needs and sufferings of others. This includes writing pieces that provoke thought, inspire change, or creating works of art that raise fundamental questions, spark conversations, or move people into action to alleviate suffering.

In conclusion, the journey to balance creativity and compassion is an ongoing process, a dynamic cycle of learning, growing, and evolving. The teachings of the Buddha provide us with a valuable roadmap, urging us towards balanced living. Applying this to our creative processes and compassionate undertakings could significantly enhance our spiritual and artistic growth, bringing a significant richness and depth to our everyday lives.

Chapter 11. Conclusion: Embracing Your Transformative Creative Journey

As we come to the end of this guide, it becomes evident that Buddha's teachings are not only insightful directions for spiritual realization but also an empowering map to our creative consciousness. This understanding unfurls the latent power within us and enables space for expression, exploration, and transformation.

11.1. Embrace Impermanence in Creativity

Creativity is not a fixed trait, but a flow, a dynamic process perpetually in flux. Buddha's teachings on the impermanence or "anicca" can be translated to our creative pursuits. Our ideas, our work, our styles evolve over time. Embrace this transience. Every creative phase you go through is a necessary step in your development. Release the attachment to outcomes, letting go of the need for your work to be perfect or everlasting. This openness to change is the cradle of creativity.

11.2. The Power of Mindfulness

Mindfulness in Buddha's teaching, or "sati," is awareness of the present moment. Rooting your consciousness in the here and now pushes the boundaries of your creative potential. It brings clarity, facilitates connection with your environment, and enables insightful reflections. The act of creation then becomes an active meditation, where your full attention is on the task, and the task becomes an extension of your being.

11.3. The Interplay of Form and Emptiness - The Heart of Creativity

The "Heart Sutra," one of Buddha's profound teachings, highlights the interplay between Form and Emptiness. In the context of creativity, Form represents the work we produce and Emptiness, the vast potentiality of ideas yet to materialize. We must come to understand that Form is Emptiness, and Emptiness is Form; our work is not separate from us or the universe but intertwined. The art created is a part of us and yet has a life of its own.

11.4. Embodying Compassion - Infusing Heart Into Your Art

Karuna, or compassion, in Buddhism is the desire to alleviate the suffering of others. As creators, we have the power to touch hearts, to stir emotions, and provoke thought. Infuse compassion into your work, for it is the mark of deeply resonating, meaningful, and transformative art. Empathy makes the message universal, more relatable for your audience, and creates an enduring impact.

11.5. Acceptance and Letting Go - Developing Creative Resilience

Life unfolds alongside suffering, or "dukkha," an essential teaching of Buddha. Similarly, the creative process is not devoid of frustrations, rejections, and failures. Developing the attitude of acceptance, acknowledging these design elements of the creative process without becoming despondent is crucial for creative resilience. Learning to let go, to not overly attach our identity to our work, helps us persist, evolve, and transform.

11.6. Integrating Creativity in Daily Life - Living Artfully

Lastly, respect the art of living. Buddha's teachings compel us to live fully and deliberately, making our very life a masterpiece. Merge the duality of life and art. Infuse creativity into the simplest of activities, making meals, having conversations, or solving problems. This blending enriches your life and spills over to enrich your work too.

As we conclude this journey through the mindful creator's landscape, note that Buddha's teachings aren't prescriptive paths to creativity but offer philosophical underpinnings to reframe your perception. The wisdom shared is not only meant to be cognitively understood but experientially realized. This guide is just the beginning. The journey of exploration, understanding, and applying Buddha's teachings to your creative endeavors is a continuum.

Immerse yourself in this transformative journey. Be open. Be patient. Allow the wisdom to permeate through you, ultimately leading you to your authentic self and the brilliant creator within. Allow this journey to facilitate self-discovery, breed novel ideas, and enrich your creative expressions. Remember, Creativity, like Enlightenment, is not a destination but a process, a beautifully unfolding journey.

Ride the waves of impermanence, nurture mindfulness, dance with the form and the formless, infuse compassion into your work, embrace the 'dukkha' of creation, and live artfully. Enlightened Creativity beckons you!

Revel in the ambiguity and celebrate the mystery, for you are on a pathless path – a journey of awakening your Creative Buddha!

9 7 9 8 8 5 6 2 3 9 0 9 5